The Avogel Tribe of Louisiana

Volume 1

By

John Sitting Bear

authorHOUSE™

1663 LIBERTY DRIVE, SUITE 200
BLOOMINGTON, INDIANA 47403
(800) 839-8640
WWW.AUTHORHOUSE.COM

First published by AuthorHouse 09/15/04

ISBN: 1-4208-0221-6 (sc)

Printed in the United States of America
Bloomington, Indiana

This book is printed on acid-free paper.

First published June 30, 1999

SEAL OF THE AVOGEL * · * GREAT

Table of Contents

FORWARD

By

Phd. Rebecca Saunders

And

Rob Mann

We are pleased to have been contacted by Chief Mayeux for the production of this book. Originally, we had hoped to contribute a chapter on the Southeastern Native American prehistory , history , and ethnogenesis, but our schedules did not permit it. This is no great loss to this volume, which stands on its own as the Avogel account of much of what we were to consider. There is much to learn within pages of this volume, in which Chief Mayeux discusses the myth, history , and the future of the Avogel people.

As Chief Mayeux discusses in Chapter 2, the Avogel once occupied the varied landscape from between the headwaters of the Teche to the Rapides of the Red River, with main villages at

Marksville and in what is now Alexandria. This "paired town" approach to regional politics is a Southeastern trait with much antiquity .The "Sacred Mound of the Main Village" at Marksville was within the Marksville site itself; the historical narrative mentions the Marksville site as "central" to the Avogel cultural landscape. Most of the site, which contains six mounds (and is currently a state park), is believed to date to between A.D. 1 and 600. However, not all of the six mounds at the site have been dated and some historic Indian use of the site has been documented. The Avogel know the location of the site in Alexandria.

The Avogel were located strategically with respect to resources. Their control of the lower Red River and the vast river and floodplain system below its' confluence with the Mississippi River positioned them to be active traders. In prehistory , their position on the Red allowed them access (directly or in down-the-line trade with the Caddo) to highly prized lithic resources in the Ozarks, which is reflected in their trade language name "the Flint People." In historic times, the Avogel expanded their inventories to include Spanish cattle and horses. Their roles as traders may help explain why the Avogel survived into the 21st century when many of their neighboring tribes did not. Studies have shown that trading peoples have great cultural resiliency and flexibility acquired through dealing with many different peoples; these characteristics have been found in many tribes that survived in the late 20th and 21st centuries.

Nevertheless, in the political manoeuvring between Native American tribes, on the one hand, and European powers on the other, not to mention the manoeuvring between representatives of these two great peoples, the Avogel were politically marginalized in the l700s, lost much of their land in the 1800s, and lost much of their population in the 19th and early 20th century. There are many competing versions of these events, but Chief Mayeux gives us an all-too-rare insight to Native American history of the time. Interspersed with comments on traditional customs used to defuse political situations, the chapter explains much about the many "strange bedfellows" that the political landscape created in the early historic period.

The Avogel believe that they were being hunted to extinction in the late 19th and early 20th century. Nevertheless, a core of traditional Avogel secretly clung to their identity and their culture, thus preserving it for subsequent generations. Chief Mayeux's family was one of these. Owing to the efforts of these families over the last 300 years, the Avogel can arise today with many of their traditions and tales intact. Without this long chain of events and efforts, this book could not have been written. It is a testimony to the will of the Flint People.

PREFACE

For many years people have been requesting information on the Avogel Tribe of La. One day, one of the members of the Tribal Council recommended that I write a book about the Tribe for the Tribe. In this way, when others who were interested in the tribe wanted information, they could purchase a copy of the book and learn whatever they wanted to know. After sifting through 8 or 10 file drawers of documentation gleaned from the Universities of Texas, Oklahoma, Indiana, and Arkansas, I put the information I felt would be of most interest to the public into this book. The Tribal Council has already informed me that they suggest that a second volume be printed in the near future that contains some of the valuable information from the files that were not put into this work. Volume 2 will be forthcoming in the near future.

Chief John Sitting Bear Mayeux

INTRODUCTION

This book is about the AVOGEL tribe of Louisiana. Avoyelles Parish in Louisiana was named for our tribe. The name AVOGEL was given to us by our allies, the Nachi. "Avo" means "flint" in their language, and "gel" means "people". We have been known by other names in other languages as well: "TASAnNNUKOGOULA" from the Biloxi language, "OKLA TASAnNNUK" by the Choctaws and Chickasaws, and "LITTLE TAENSA" from a misunderstanding of who we were by Iberville 1699-1700. It must be remembered that the "art of spelling" had not yet been invented by the Europeans when they arrived here and that is why in many instances with the same author, we sometimes see the same name spelled different ways. Because of our friendship and close ties to the Nachi, we still call ourselves the "AVOGEL!" Since the time of the French occupation, the spelling has been changed to "Avoyel" because the "g" sound in the name was difficult for them to pronounce. They also, already had a word "avoyel" for a poisonous snake, with which they were familiar .and therefore used this more familiar spelling to refer to our people. Even though the Roman alphabet does not contain a character to represent the "g" sound of the Nachi or of our language, we still use it in the name. The letter "y" in the Roman alphabet usually has a long "e" sound or the German "ya" sound. The long "e" sound is frequently represented by the letter "i" in modern English, and other European languages. The "ya" structure does not exist in our language at all!

We were given the name "The Flint People" because we traded flint to the other tribes in Louisiana and later to the Europeans for their muskets. The flints we traded came from Arkansas since very little stone is found in Louisiana. We would trade either the raw flint or flint items. We also traded horses and cattle, which we obtained in New Spain, to the French and other tribes. Because of our trading practices we were known throughout Southeastern North America.

Today some authors claim that we no longer exist and have been absorbed by other tribes. While it is true that over the centuries, our numbers have declined due to intermarriages, first with other tribes, and then with other immigrants; we are still a united people, we DO still exist as a tribe, and we have NEVER formed a confederation or conglomeration with any other tribe or tribes. We are simply the "AVOGEL" as we always have been!

This book is an attempt to tell you who we are and from where we have come. We hope our stories (which have been handed down from generation to generation) will entertain and help you to understand us as a people. We are proud of our heritage and are proud to count ourselves among the "American People!"

Today, at the beginning of the 21st century, we number 238 people. We have been in hiding for a long time due to the excesses that have been visited on the indigenous people of the Americas. We are coming out of hiding at this time because we feel that it may be safe enough to let others know of our presence.

ACKNOWLEDGE MENTS

I dedicate this book to the memory of my Mother, Azema Marie Brouillette Mayeux, and my AVOGEL ancestors. I appreciate their teaching me the ways, customs, medicinal remedies, and the history of their times.

My mother Azema Marie Brouillette Mayeux, my grandmother Alice Roy Mayeux, taught me everything they knew about medicine plants and ways to treat illnesses. My grandfather, son of Joseph Mayeux, taught me how to hunt with a blowgun and how to make "Indian" toys. Our customs and ways and language were taught to me by my mother and father who had learned it from their parents and relatives. It was my Aunt Nini who told me about our ancestoral line from old Colfa to Old Chief Joseph to the other chiefs of our time.

CHIEFS OF THE AVOGEL

Azema Marie Brouillette Mayeux was chief from 1927 until her tragic death in 1975. Before her, our chief was Joseph Mayeux, son of Pierre and Josephine (greatgrandson of Old Chief Joseph dates unknown), 1895 to 1896; before him was Azema Charrier Marcotte (granddaughter of Tsugande Charrier), who was chief from 1885 to 1895. Before her was Old Chief Joseph (greatgrandfather of Chief Joseph Mayeux) who lived to almost 100 years old and led the Avogel wisely. The Storyteller says he was a descendant of Old Chief Colfa who was in the battle to drive out the Spaniards under the leadership of DeSoto. Some even claim that it was he who killed DeSoto, but we have no way of proving this.

I wish to express my thanks and gratitude also
to PhD. Rebecca Saunders
Curator of the Anthropology Museum of
Natural Science
And
Rob Mann, Regional Archaeology Program,
Southeast Louisiana
LOUISIANA STATE UNIVERSITY

Without whose help and encouragement this book would not have been possible!!!

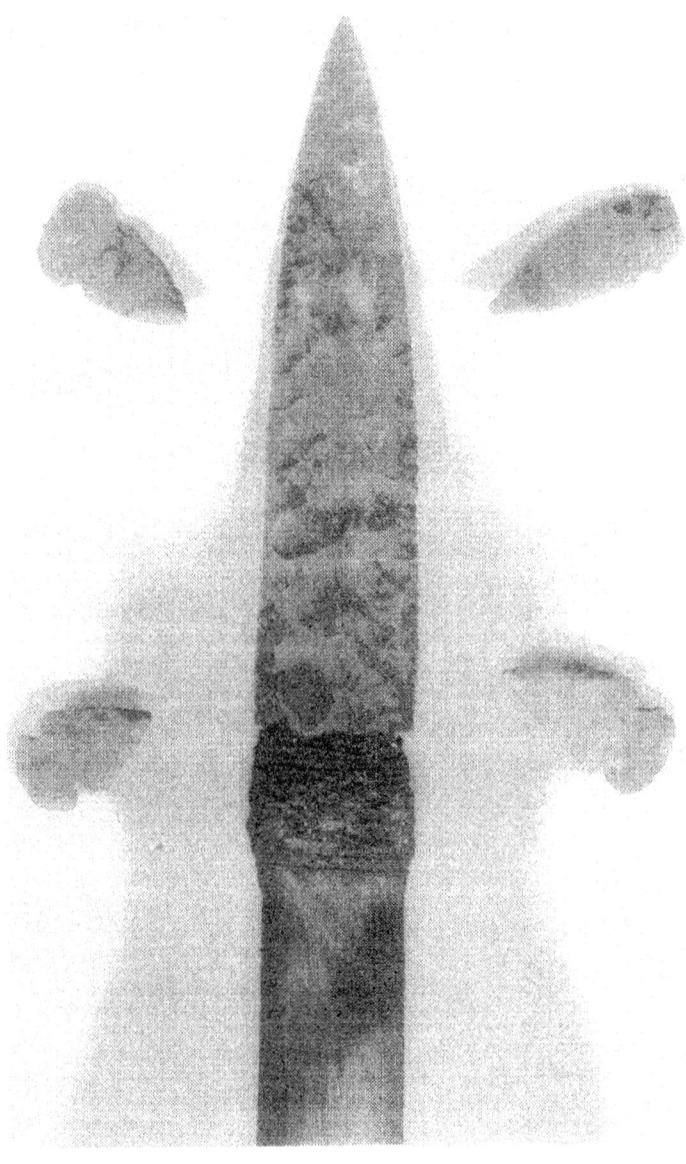

CHAPTER 1
PREHISTORY

The Story of Creation

In the beginning, the Creator made all things, large and small, seen and unseen. In those days, the animals and the humans could talk to each other and understood each other's speech. Our Holy Men tell us today that the animals still speak to us; but, the reason we do not understand them anymore is that we are just too busy and in too great of a hurry to listen to them.

The Creator placed all the humans in a large cave under the earth near a large lake. Here He cared for them and fed them every day. They wanted for nothing! You see, the Creator had commanded the people to eat and drink as much as they needed each day to live comfortably; but, not to keep any of the leftovers! At the end of each day, the Creator came and removed the leftovers and each morning He brought fresh food and water for the people.

Then, one day, Spider, the Trickster, came and spoke to the humans. He told them that the Creator was always very busy and that one day He may forget to feed the people. At first, they refused to listen to his words; but, as time passed and he continued to repeat his warning, doubt began to grow in the minds of the people. Fearing that Spider may be right, the people asked what he suggested they do to prevent hunger and thirst in case the Creator forgot them in his hurry. He told them to hide just a little of the leftovers each day, and then they would have what they needed in case the Creator forgot them or was delayed in taking care of them.

The people argued among themselves; some said that they should continue to follow the laws of the Creator, while others argued that they should follow Spider's advice. These people were greedy. They took it upon themselves to hide some of the leftovers each day against the time when the Creator would forget about them and they would be hungry and thirst. This was the first disagreement among the people and they were divided.

When the Creator saw that some of the food was being hoarded against his wishes, He became angry and roared that He would destroy the humans for not following His will. Upon hearing the Creator's decision to destroy the humans, Bear, who had always been a true friend to the humans, went to the Creator and told Him about Spider's lies and how the humans had been deceived. When Bear had finished his story, Creator changed His decision to destroy the humans; but decided that they could no longer live in the cave. Bear suggested that they be placed in his care and he would teach them how to live on the surface of the earth. He would teach them how to hunt, plant, and gather their food. He would teach them how to build their shelters and how to live with the other animals and with Nature. Creator thought about this and found Bear's suggestion a good one. The next day Bear led the humans out of the cave and up onto the surface of the earth. Immediately after they had left, Creator caused a great earthquake and sealed the entrance of the cave forever! The easy life that the humans had enjoyed since the beginning of time was over. Now they would have to work for all that they had. Also, now, they would grow old in time and eventually die.

Bear stayed with the humans near the large lake for a few days to let them rest, and then began to move them South until they came to a large river. This river had a reddish tint to the water because of the soil, and so Bear named this river the Red River, and told the people that this was a good place to live. Everything they needed to live was nearby. He told them that the land further to the south was marshy and not as good as the riverbanks.

Here, they built their homes, and Bear kept his promise to the Creator. He showed the humans how to fish, hunt, and forage for food, both plants and animals, and how to care for their young. For providing them with food, the humans promised Mother Earth that they would only use what they needed to live healthily and no more. This was also done to show the Creator that they remembered what He had done for them and their love for Him. Bear spoke to the animals and explained to them also that they were to be hunted for food and shelter for humans; but not our of meanness. This is why, even today, animals give themselves to hunters for their bodies to be used as food. Bear also instructed the people to help each other, and to treat each other with dignity and respect, and to respect all living things. This is the way to live in peace.

As the centuries passed, the people became many and could not all live together. Therefore, it was decided that once they had grown to a certain number, some would volunteer to move away where there would still be enough food and nourishment for all. As these people moved away, they called themselves by new names. After a time, some had moved so far away, that their language began to change too. This is why today there are many languages and not just one. At first, almost all the tribes of humans called themselves "the people" in their new languages; but later some of them decided to use other words that they felt better described who they were and how they lived. They also changed and varied their customs with their new languages; but they still remembered that they were human beings.

By the time of the first European contact, the Avogel land was bounded on the East by the Great River, Malbanchia (Mississippi River), to the North by Black Bayou, to the West as far as "Les Rapides" (Alexandria, La.), and to the South we controlled the upper HAnCHAFALAY A (Atchafalaya), which means "The Long River" (in the Trade Language of the Eastern tribes), from "Three Rivers" to the head waters of the Bayou Teche. To the Southwest where the Okelousa people who were our friends.

The Gift of the Pipe and Ceremonies

At first, the people lived in peace and harmony; but after a while they began to change and to become selfish. They were forgetting the lesson they had learned when they were living in the Great Cave with the Creator. They killed more animals than they needed for food, stored more food than they needed for leaner times, and treated one another in a mean and shameful way. They had forgotten how to talk to the Creator and the animals were pleading with the Creator to stop their wicked ways.

One day, three young men, who liked to bully others, were hunting buffalo on the prairie, and they saw a cloud coming toward them. This cloud or fog turned into a beautiful, white buffalo. This was a sight that none of them had ever seen before. When the White Buffalo was near them, it changed into a beautiful young woman. As she came near, they recoiled in fear.

When she stood before them, she told them that she was a messenger from the Creator and that she was coming to the village with a gift of great value for the people. Before she could bring the treasure, however, the people had to build a large mound where all the people could gather together, and in the center of the mound they were to build a shelter for the treasure she was bringing. When the mound and the building were finished, she would come and meet with the people.

One of the young warriors, greedier than the rest, began to plan how to steal this treasure and keep it for himself. The Spirit knew his thoughts and with a frightening glance turned him into dust. The other two hunters promised to deliver her message to the Chief and the Council and immediately mounted their horses and left the young woman on the prairie.

The hunters kept their word and returned to the village and told the Council everything that had happened. The people built the mound and waited for the appearance of the young woman. Not long after the completion of the mound, the White Buffalo was seen coming toward the village, and again it changed into the beautiful young maiden that the hunters had described. The Chief met her at the entrance to the village, along with the Tribal Council, and welcomed her. She then instructed the Chief and the Council to gather the people and follow her to the mound. She ascended the mound from the East and instructed the people to form a circle on the mound, moving in a clockwise manner. The Chief and the Council were to sit before the entrance of the shelter at the center of the mound. This entrance faced east, as she had instructed, and there were no other openings in the structure. Everyone waited for the young woman to speak and all were eager to see what treasures she had brought them. She then told them to be seated.

Once they were all seated, she began to unwrap the package she had brought with her which had been wrapped in a red colored animal skin. In it was the Calumet, tobacco, and a beaded bag. She then addressed the people and told them that the way they had been living was not the way the Creator wanted them to live. The Pipe and the tobacco were His gifts to them so that they could talk to the Creator directly. The smoke from the Pipe would carry their words to the Creator, and he would hear everything they said and would judge their words as being true or false. If their words were true, He would protect them; but, if their words were false, He would punish them! This was to be the same for anyone who smoked the Calumet. The Pipe was always to be passed in a clockwise way when several were to smoke the Pipe. The Pipe could be smoked by anyone; this was a gift to the people and not just tribal leaders. It could be smoked by outsiders as well.

In the beaded bundle were sacred objects sent by the Creator to protect the people. The beads on the Sacred Bundle formed the sign of the Dragonfly. It was explained to the People that this was the guiding spirit of their tribe and that it would watch over them for as long as they survived as a people. The other items in the Sacred Bundle cannot be discussed here; but they are still kept safe even to this day.

As long as they preserved this Pipe and Sacred Bundle, the People would continue to exist even during the worst of times. The treasures were then put in a place of honor inside of the shelter they had built. Six men were chosen to guard the items and insure that they were used properly.

Then she began to instruct the People in the ways that the Creator wanted them to live together. She told them all that the Creator had instructed her to say to them. These words became the law of the People. Since these words came from the Creator, one person was chosen among the Tribe to remember the laws and teach

14

them to the young, and pass them on to another when his time to die had come. The same was to be done by the six Guardians of the Sacred Items.

With the treasure and the laws, she also brought ceremonies to the People. These ceremonies were the Fire Ceremony, the Making of Relatives Ceremony, the Corn Ceremony, the Making of Peace Ceremony, the Marriage Ceremony, and the Burial Ceremony. There was one last word of caution about the gifts given to the People by the Creator, "If any of these were ever abused or misused, the People would cease to exist!"

The young maiden stayed with the People for a while to answer any questions they had, and to make sure that they followed the will of the Creator. After she had satisfied herself that they understood all that had been told to them, she turned again into the White Buffalo and left the People. As she was about to leave their sight, a fog enveloped her and they saw her no more.

THE GENTLE PEOPLE

In the days of the grandfathers' grandfathers, there lived a large tribe to the east of the Avogel lands who called themselves "The Gentle People" in their language. They lived on the eastern side of the great river that ran north and south (Malbanchia). These people were great friends of the Avogel. We lived in peace and harmony with them for a very long time.

One day, one of the Elders among the Gentle People called for a gathering of the whole tribe. During the night he had had a vision. In this vision, his spirit guide told him that the Creator was giving a new land to the Gentle People far to the North, near to where the Great River that runs north and south starts its journey. It was decided, that since this Elder was a holy man, that the tribe must follow the vision and go to the land promised them by the Creator. They began making preparations for the long journey.

16

In his vision, he was told to follow the river and that the People would be shown where to cross.

When the day came to leave, all the tribe assembled at the main village. Some of the clans did not want to leave and so they stayed in their lands; but, almost all decided to follow the Elder and with their backs to the sea (Gulf of Mexico) they prepared to leave.

We, the Avogel, were heartbroken when we heard about the vision and the decision to leave the land. Our wonderful neighbors and relatives, for some of our people had married with the Gentle People, would be leaving us for good. We could not imagine life without them! If it was the will of the Creator; however, we could only accept His decision and not question it. We had decided to make two spears with flint heads, one from each of our great villages, to protect the Gentle People on their journey and to remember us, the friends they left behind. We presented the spears to them on the day they began their journey to the North. We never heard from them

17

again, although today we suspect who they may be from stories we have heard.

In Mari Sandoz's book <u>Crazy Horse,</u> in the story of a raiding party by the Oglala against the Crows, Brave-Man tells this story: "So it was done, and just before they left, the people put a great honor upon Crazy Horse and his friend, He Dog, one not given to anyone for many years -they were not only made lance-bearers of the Crow-Owners society, which was good but were given the care of the two lances of the Oglalas, the two lances that had been with the people longer than any man could remember. Surely it was far back beyond the Missouri, Worm and Old Bad Heart Bull thought. No one remembered, either, how they came except that they were given to the people as a sign that their strength and power should live again as the grass in the spring when the brave warriors carried the lances into battle in enemy country ." It is believed today from this story told by Brave-Man that these are the Gentle People of the old days.

The few of the Gentle People who stayed with us in the South helped our sense of loneliness to a small extent. These few watched over the graves of the grandfathers, the Old Ones, and kept their language and customs. Many of their traditions, ceremonies, and beliefs were very similar to our own. Maybe this was one of the reasons we remained close to them and always counted them as friends and family.

NEW COMERS MOVE IN

The Nachi

(Natchez)

The Nachi were a strange people to us when we first met them. They came out of the South. The first group of them came over the Sea from the South in boats. They found the Great River that runs north and south, and went up the river to a high place just past the Red River where we lived. Other tribes were afraid of the new comers for they were very aggressive and loved nothing more than a good fight.

It was said that their Great Chief, who was called the Great Sun, was a direct descendent of the Sun itself, and that he would come with the rest of his people some time later. Some years later, more of the Nachi came overland from the southwest and moved in with their people, and among them was the Great Sun.

We became friends with the Nachi from the very beginning. Since we were one of the oldest tribes in the area, they sought our wisdom and knowledge; especially about the other tribes. They realized that since we had been trading with most of the tribes in the Southeast and were on friendly terms with all of them, that we were valuable allies to have. They also regarded us as kindred since we were very similar to them in physical appearance. We were about the same height and build and we were born "white" just as they were. Marriage between our people was encouraged by both tribes. At the same time, a strong, friendly nation like the Nachi could help to protect our dwindling, older tribe. Many marriages over the years with people of other tribes had caused our numbers to decrease. This brought a fear that one day we might cease to exist as a people. Their protection, however, lasted only until the French destroyed the Nachi in a war. The few survivors that escaped capture were scattered among the various tribes.

It was said that the Nachi had left great temples made of stone when they were driven out of their old homeland to the South before coming to live on the east side of the Malbanchia. They decided to build mounds of earth as we had done, to replace their temples that they had left behind. Since most of their priests had been killed by the enemy in their civil war, which forced them to leave, most of their secret religious teachings had been lost. Only a few old men knew the stories of the old days and those had gaps in them. Some men and women were considered spiritual leaders; but they could not do the things priests were supposed to do as was told in the old stories.

The Nachi were also quick to adapt to some of our ways too; but, we, on the other hand, could not accept some of their ways. For example, the killing of children and other tribal members to accompany the dead chiefs on their journey to the after life was something we could not accept.

Life was too precious to us, especially the life of children.

Chata/Chica

In the days of the grandfathers' grandfathers, there came a new people to take the place of the Gentle People who had left to go to the North. One day, an unknown scout was seen coming from the direction of the setting sun to our land. When questioned, he told us that his people had left their land at the edge of the Great Western Sea, where the sun goes to sleep, and had been traveling for a long time. They had done this because of a vision that came to one of their elders in which the Creator had promised them a new land. When the elder asked where this land was to be, the Creator told him that He would show him the way. At dusk each day, he was to plant his staff in the earth, and each morning, whichever way the staff would lean, that would be the way to go. When the staff would remain upright, then that would be the sign that they had arrived at the land promised them.

When their Council had heard of the vision, the decision was made to follow the words of the Creator. They journeyed for a very long time, and each day the staff would lean to the East.

At first, this news caused concern among the Avogel. What if our land was the land promised to these people? We were a much smaller tribe and greatly outnumbered. When they asked permission to pass through our land and presented us with presents, we came to understand that they were to move farther East across the great Malbanchia. We were happy to give them permission and even helped them to find the best place to cross and we provided them with boats and rafts as well. During their brief stay with us, we helped them with provisions for their journey and smoked the Calumet and pledged our friendship one to the other .

Some time later, we heard that the Sacred Staff had finally shown them the place that had been promised. It was the land that had once been inhabited by the Gentle People. Although this brought back painful memories, we understood that this was the wish of the Creator and that there was a reason for all that had happened.

This tribe was very large, too large for them to all live in one area for they would eventually use up all the game and good resources. The decision was made for half of them to move a way farther where Mother Earth could provide enough for all the people; but no one wanted to leave the beautiful new country. So, to decide the matter, it was agreed that a stickball game would be played to see who move and who would stay. One team was led by a great leader named Chata, and the other team was led by his brother, also a great leader, Chica. When the game was over, Chata's team had won and so they would stay and Chica and his followers would move a little more north and east of this place. There they would have sufficient food to survive and flourish. In time, Chata's people came to be known as Choctaw, and Chica' s people as Chickasaw. Even today, if one studies the languages of these two people, the similarities can be found that show that they have a common base.

Numbering so many people also made their influence great among the other tribes. The trade language that eventually developed in the Southeast of North America was based on many of the words from their language. This may be why duPratz, in his book The History of Louisiana, stated that the trade language was based on the Chichasaw's language.

In later years, in more recent history , many Choctaws came and settled in Louisiana because of the abundant food sources and friendly relationship with the Avogel and other Louisiana tribes. Another reason for settling in Louisiana was due to European and later American pressures. Each tried to use the Choctaw to their own advantage to acquire land that was not theirs to take. Today, many places in Louisiana have Choctaw names.

Conclusion

In the time before the arrival of the Europeans, we had heard that many nations had moved to new locations; but, we were still on our own land and had not been moved. Years later, with the coming of the Europeans, many more nations left their ancestral lands and moved west of the Malbanchia, some came to Louisiana.

It had always been our custom to welcome new comers and visitors to our land and villages, and to hide until enemies who outnumbered us left. This has always been our way and this is one of the reasons that we still survive to this day in spite of what has happened to other indigenous people in the Americas. We may be few in number today; but, we do still exist and we will survive. We still look out for each other and insure that the tribe continues. We still have the gifts of the Creator in our possession, and to them we have

John Sitting Bear

added those items given to us by the French and Spanish as signs of friendship.

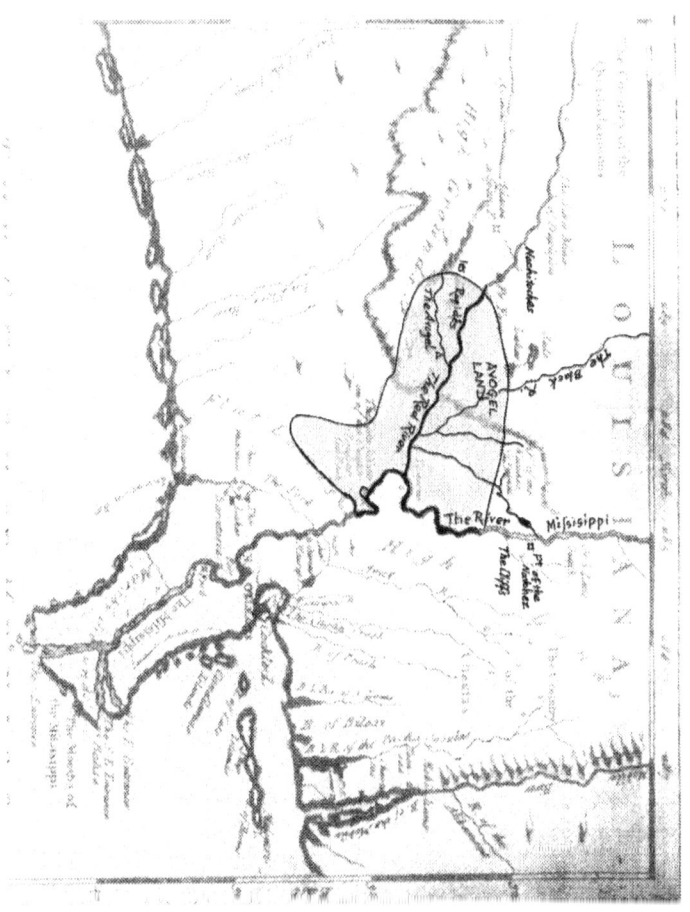

CHAPTER 2 History

THE FRENCH PERIOD

What we call the "French Period" is that period of history from the time that Europeans first came into our lands and until the French gave Louisiana to the Spanish at the end of the French and Indian War.

Our first contact with Europeans, according to our oral history, is when DeSoto and his men came pillaging through North America. Under the leadership of the great War Chief Colfa, our people, the AVOGEL, united with many other tribes and attacked DeSoto and his men and succeeded in killing him along with many of his men. This attack was also due to the fact that his men had raided our Main Village, raped some of the women who were caught and killed all others that they found. Many had escaped into the woods when word of their coming was given. We had heard from other survivors of other tribes where these men had been before, as to how they had treated the people. We were anxious to rid ourselves of these people who killed so many and had so little respect for life. This is the reason we followed the great War Chief Colfa into battle. We are a peaceful people, and if we can resolve differences with peaceful means we will do so, or we will scatter and hide until the unreasonable people become discouraged and leave our land.

From that time until the end of the 17th Century, a few Europeans, mainly hunters and trappers came into our territory. .They were few and behaved like human beings, so we welcomed them and treated them accordingly. The AVOGEL are first mentioned by the Europeans under Iberville in 1699-1700, when he calls them the "Little Taensas". At this time, according to Iberville, the AVOGEL numbered about 280 persons with approximately 40 being warriors. This information was based on the few people he met in one village and was applied to the whole nation. Even the term he used to identify us was typical of the Europeans at this time.

For some strange reason, I guess it was because they felt that they were superior to the indigenous people they found in the area, they made many mistakes in using the names we had given things and places. Their French language also contributed to some of these "mistakes". For instance, the Trade Language name for a small river was "bogue" which they changed to "bayou". The "Hatchafalaya" River became the "Atchafalaya" River to the French. The "AVOGEL" became the "Avoyel" Nation. Another reason for changing the spelling was due to the word avoyel which was a small poisonous snake in the French

33

language, and some of the first settlers thought that these people had named themselves after this snake. In time, they found that this was not true, but the damage had been done and the misspelling remained. The name "AVOGEL" comes from the Nachi (Natchez Nation), our allies. "Avo" in their language means "flint", while "gel" (pronounced /zhell) means "people". We were known as the "Flint People" because of our trade in flint with the other tribes and later with the French. We would go north and obtain flint and bring it back to Gulf Coast Area and there, trade the raw flint or the finished projectile points, knife blades, or lance heads, to the people in the area. For this reason also, we were known as the "TASAnNNUKO GOULA"; "TASAnNNUK" meaning "flint" and "goula" meaning people or nation in the Southeastern Trade Language. Again, this demonstrates how words with the "g" were used to denote "people" or "nations" and not the European "y" as we find so many times in our contact with Europeans. It should also be noted here that the "Indian" listing of American Tribes of the Genealogical Society also spells the name of the Tribe as "AVOGEL ".

The Europeans always insisted that we learn their language, which was no big deal for us since we spoke several languages; but they appeared to be unwilling to learn ours. I believe it was the superiority attitude they had about themselves. It was their way of justifying their taking of our lands and goods by claiming to "civilize" us to their ways. What is interesting is that they would never have survived their early years in this country without our "primitive and barbaric" help. The mosquitoes alone would have killed them during the summer months here. Without our help, they may have eaten poisonous plants and died. In fact, in later years, many came to our "medicine men" to cure them of ailments they had that their own European doctors could not cure.

In 1718, M. LePage DuPratz came to Lower Louisiana as an agent of the King of France to watch over the King's Plantation. He wrote profusely about what he saw and experienced. In his book, translated into English years later in London, The History of Louisiana. Book IV, "Of the Natives of Louisiana", Chapter II, Section II, "Of the Nations inhabiting on the West of the Mississippi", he states, "From the Oque-Loussas to the Red River, we meet with no other nation; but upon the banks of this river, a little about the Rapid, is seated the small nation of the Avoyels (sic). These are the people who bring to our settlers horses, oxen, and cows. I know not in what fair they buy them, nor with what money they pay for them; but the truth is, they sell them to us for about seventeen shillings a-piece. The Spaniards of New-Spain have such numbers of them that they do not know what to do with them, and are obliged to those who will take them off their hands. At present the French have a greater number of them than they want, especially of horses."

DuPratz goes on to describe the AVOGEL as being born "white". Then as they spend more time in the open and also due to the use of bear grease, which helps keep the insects away, their skin color becomes darker. They use their dwellings to sleep and store their belongings or to get out of the bad weather. They live in the open as much as is possible. It was due to this reason that modern AVOGEL could "pass for white" by covering their skin with clothing and wearing a hat to keep from turning "darker".

The history of the AVOGEL is tied to the history of the Tonica and the Biloxi. In M. DuPratz's book he also states that: "..., a nation of two thousand warriors makes war upon and violently pursues another nation of five hundred warriors, who retire among a nation in alliance with their enemies. If this last nation adopt the five hundred, the first nation, though two thousand in number, immediately lay down their arms, and instead of continuing hostilities, reckon the adopted nation among the number of their

37

allies." This fact is important in understanding the connection of the AVOGEL and the Tonica/ Biloxi. In the early 1700s, the renewal of the Chickasaw raids forced the Tonica from their village on the Yazoo River (approximately 1706) and they received permission from the Homa to settle near them opposite the mouth of the Red River. During the next two years, tensions grew until they attacked the Homa and drove them south. Taking the hunting lands from the Homa however, caused a dispute over hunting grounds and boundary lines between the Nachi (Natchez), a great ally of the AVOGEL, and the Tonica. These disputes eventually led to a war between the Nachi and the Toncia. The Nachi were about to destroy the Tonica when they came to the AVOGEL and asked them to intercede on their behalf and stop the war. It was this intercession and the custom mentioned above that saved the Tonica from extinction. They, the Tonica, were forced to give up the Homa land and live with the AVOGEL, as a condition of ending the war.

Once the Tonica moved out of the Homa lands, the Biloxi moved into the old Homa Indian Village which today is known as Angola, Louisiana.

Later, in a war with the French, the Nachi were destroyed and without our allies to support us, the Tonica with the help of the European descendents in the area began to drive us from our land and force us to hide once more to survive.

It is important to mention here also, that during the attack by the Nachi on Fort Rosalie which had been occupied and held by the French, two "Europeans": Mayeux and Lebeau were allowed to leave the Fort alive while everyone else had been massacred. According to their stories told to the French, they had been allowed to live for different reasons. However, since the objective of the Nachi was to kill and drive all the French out of Lower Louisiana, it is hard to accept that they would allow two Frenchmen to live unless there was something about them that would allow them to be set free. These men had

"Indian" blood and were considered family and friends by the Nachi and they were "let loose".

During the French period, many of the AVOGEL were baptized into the Catholic Church in the town of Mansura, La. Most of these people had only one European name such as "Joseph". To be baptized into the Church, they needed a "sponsor", someone, of Catholic European descent, who could confirm or attest that the "Indian" knew their religion and would be a "good" Catholic. Many times, after baptism, the "Indian" was given the last name of the "sponsor" or took the name for themselves so that they would have two European names like the rest of the Church community .The Catholic Church in Mansura, La. did something else that no other registrar had done or would do in the future: they recorded each baptized "Indian" on a separate list and then if the "Indian" was not AVOGEL, they would list the Tribe to which they belonged. In this way, Tonica, Ofo, etc. and AVOGEL were properly recorded in the Church records. If no name of a Tribe was given, it was understood that the "Indian" was AVOGEL, otherwise, the respective Tribe was recorded next to the name of the individual. Most of the family names chosen by our people or given to them by the French Catholic Church were Mayeux, Marcotte, LeBoeuf, Guillory , and Charrier .

In the first half of the 18th century the name of the Chief of the AVOGEL was Joseph Mayeux, a son of the first Joseph Mayeux to come to Louisiana and an "Indian" mother (legend has it that she was Avogel). It is said that this is the same Mayeux that had been allowed to live during the attack on Fort Rosalie by the Nachi. It was also during this time that many AVOGEL were killed by local citizens and their land taken from them. In those days it was more dangerous to kill someone's dog or chicken than to kill an "Indian".

In his book dated 1723, M. DuPratz states that the AVOGEL land extended west from the Mississippi River (Malbanchia) along both sides of the Red River to just above the Rapides (present day Alexandria), and south from the Mississippi / Red River (called Three Rivers today) along the Atchafalaya (Hatcha Falaya) River to the headwaters of the Teche, and north to Black Bayou. There were two main villages; one at present day Marksville, which was the main village, and the other at present day Alexandria. He did not mention the other minor villages spread throughout the AVOGEL lands. All of this land was stolen or "purchased" from the AVOGEL whether they wanted to part with it or not!!!

THE SPANISH PERIOD

This was the time of great suffering and hardship, when many of our people were murdered without just cause. This time is also called the Second Coming of the Hornheads. This name was given to the Spanish soldiers because of the helmets they wore. Our first encounter with these Hornheads had been under deSoto and his men. Due to this first encounter, our people were not happy when they learned that the Spanish had been given the territory of Louisiana. We had also heard the stories of how the Spanish had treated the "Indians" of Mexico, with whom we used to trade and the "Natives" of the other Spanish lands, i.e. California, Mexico, etc. The "trading" we had done with the Comanches and the horses and cattle we had procured from "New Spain", also did not put us in good standing with the Spanish. They had old scores to settle, and settle they did!

In October 1764, Spain officially took over the colony of la Louisiane, which had been given by the King of France to this cousin the King of Spain for the love he held for him. This also was part of the agreement that ended the French and Indian War between France and England. This move ended the French colonial period in North America with a few small exceptions of some islands that France was allowed to retain.

On 21 May 1765, Antonio de Ulla was named governor of la Louisiane with instructions to change nothing in the colonial government. In addition, the treaty which had gifted the King of Spain with la Louisiane, carried a requirement that all treaties with the "natives" be honored and continued under Spanish rule. Ulla arrived 22 February 1766 in North America and at la Nouvelle Orleans on 5 March 1766. On 20 January 1767 he signed the transfer document, officially transferring la Louisiane to Spain.

The French of Louisiana did not want the Spanish to take over and had petitioned the King of France to resend his "gift"; but to no avail. In 1768, at la Nouvelle Orleans, began an uprising by the French citizens. This was not done because of incompetence or mishandling of the laws by Ulla; this was done in an effort to remove the Spanish rule. The French government had been so corrupt for so long that the French did not want to change things. Ulla had decided to rule evenly and fairly with everyone and took steps to stop the corruption. This did not sit well with the French citizens who were used to favoritism and bribes allowed under the old French rule. In 1769, Ulla was recalled and a new governor was named, O'Reilly. He was sent to la Louisiane with new orders and 3000 soldiers to carry them out, along with a flotilla of 24 boats. This uprising was not going to continue and the French citizens would learn that the Spanish were determined to rule this colony like a business and turn a profit for Spain in the process. Thus the Spanish Period began.

This period of Louisiana history is also the darkest part of the history of the AVOGEL Tribe of La. The Spanish governor signed new treaties with the "Indian" tribes, which more or less guaranteed the lands and articles of friendship that they had had with the French. New treaties were signed and swords given as a sign of continued friendship. These were the official actions of the Spanish; however, the Spanish remembered the AVOGEL and their past trading practices and set about repaying them. Unofficially, the Spanish encouraged the Tonica to round up the AVOGEL, and "get rid of them" by whatever means necessary, while the Spanish government looked the other way.

In a last battle between the "traditional" AVOGEL and the "others" supported by their new allies the Tonica, on the Sacred Mound of the Main Village, the "traditionals" were forced to flee into the nearby woods to save their lives. There they remained for many years hiding out in the hopes of one day regaining their lands.

They kept their stories, their culture, their language, the sacred bundle, the pipe, and the sword given them by the French when they had signed a treaty with that nation. It was decided at that time that the AVOGEL would never speak their language with people outside of the Tribe, so that this part of their culture could never be taken from them. They believed, and rightly so, that the "others" who had joined the Tonica would eventually forget their language and become more like the Tonica and the Europeans they admired so much.

Then, the Tonica, with the help of some European settlers, began to hunt down the AVOGEL wherever they were found and many were killed. These killings were made to look like accidents or at least the records of deaths were falsified to make them look like accidents. This practice continued well into the American period. The AVOGEL who conspired with the Tonica were allowed to remain in Main Village and were eventually absorbed by the Tonica. The names of these people will always be remembered by the "Traditionals" and will be known as traitors to the people. These "traitors" took Spanish surnames and lived among the Tonica and the "Whites"; some even married with freed slaves. These people were usually referred to as "Free People of Color".

These "turncoats" were allowed to stay with the Tonica as a means of justifying the taking of AVOGEL lands. The Tonica thereafter claimed that they had "absorbed" the AVOGEL and added their lands to the Tonica holdings. They made sure that the records showed that the "turncoats" were the "only" AVOGEL that could be found. This was another reason for scattering the AVOGEL. The AVOGEL did; however, continue to meet in secret and keep their customs, language, and traditions alive. The sacred bundle and pipe were still held by the "keeper" and has remained in the possession of the "Traditional AVOGEL" from that time.

The "Traditional AVOGEL" took French names and tried to live as their French neighbors did, building homes and farms just like the people around them, and tried to "fit in" with the society of the times. The harassment by the Tonica and Spanish did not end however; but continued into the 20th century. Periodically, the Tonica with the help of the "turncoats" and "white settlers" would kill and steal any lands held by the "Traditional AVOGEL" who were still alive. These were lands that others wanted and the AVOGEL refused to sell what they had worked so hard for, for so long.

This was the Dark Age of the AVOGEL and those who survived. We did as we always had, hid and hoped that things would change. It was called the "Dark Age" because of the number of premature deaths that occurred, and the decimation of our people.

The death of Joseph Mayeux, Chief of the AVOGEL, caused the tribe to select a new leader. This new leader was a woman named Azema, who later married a white man named Charrier. She held the tribe together into the American Period. She had been given the name of a famous ancestor who had been a leader in the tribe as was the custom among the Avogel.

It was at this time that contact with the Second Village People of Les Rapides was lost and many of our relatives became unknown to us. We still search for them today.

THE AMERICAN PERIOD

With the coming of the American Period in 1803, the AVOGEL still did not feel safe or secure in their own lands. One of our elders tells of an attack on an AVOGEL family in this way. "When the "whites" and the Tonica came, they fired into the house and ordered everyone out. The children hid under the skirts of the mother so that they could not be seen. The husband was killed and the woman was told to leave or she would be killed too and to say nothing as to who had done this or she would be hunted down and killed as well. Having masks on their faces, she was able to comply without lieing.

At this time laws were passed that forbid "Indians" to marry white women on penalty of death. These men could be hanged on the spot when captured without benefit of trial or council. As far as we know, this law has never been repealed. This caused several families to constantly keep on the move and living in the back-country of Avoyelles Parish to prevent the killing of Avogel men. It was acceptable however, for "white" men to take "Indian" wives if they wanted. They were looked "down" upon socially, but the children were considered to be mostly "white". Still, they could only marry other "half-breeds" or "Indians" without being hunted down and killed outright.

Shortly after the end of the Civil War, there was a concerted effort to wipe out the AVOGEL who still existed. Over 500 of our people were rounded up by the "whites" with the help of the Tonica, placed on rail cars, and taken into the backwoods of Avoyelles Parish, and hanged. This freed more land for the "whites" and caused the remaining AVOGEL to deny publicly that they were of AVOGEL or of "Indian" descent. They still, however; met in secret and kept the customs, language, and traditions alive when they gathered for funerals, weddings, or any "family" gatherings. Their identity , and all that had happened were whispered to the young and they were admonished never to divulge who they were or that they had "Indian" blood for fear of being murdered. Some, however; like the descendants of Chief Joseph Mayeux, were remembered and not allowed to "fit-in" like the other AVOGEL who had managed to survive.

With the death of Azema Charrier Marcotte (granddaughter of Tsugande Charrier) 1885-1895, the next leader of the AVOGEL was Joseph Mayeux, a great grandson of old Chief Joseph Mayeux (his father and mother were Pierre and Josephine Mayeux). He held the position until 1896, when he was murdered one weekend by three, drunk, white men on an "Indian Hunting Trip." This meant that they would hunt and kill the first "Indian" they encountered. Unfortunately for Joseph Mayeux, he was the one they found. It was dark and a storm was coming, so Joseph decided to go to the barn and see about his animals. The three men rode up and shot him in the back and killed him. The death report later stated that he had died accidently when a brick chimney fell on him during a lightning storm. While it is true that lightning can do strange things, it has never been recorded where it changed a mud chimney to brick before knocking it down to the ground. Mayeux had a mud chimney!! His wife Julia was deceased not long after, yet no official document on her death can be found. Some say she died of pneumonia; however, in the family it was said that she too was killed because she wanted the record set straight and wanted her land given back to her and her children. Their son, my grandfather, was an orphan at the age of 9 years. He was taken in by the neighbors and allowed to work for room and board. The same was done to the other Mayeux children as they were scattered around the parish to work for their survival.

The position was next filled by Azema Marie Brouillette Mayeux until her accidental death in 1975. Although the tribe stayed active as a "family", it was not until 1997 that a new chief was selected by the tribe, Milburn John Mayeux. He is the current chief of the tribe as of the printing of this book.

In the last part of the 1970's, with the birth of the American Indian Movement throughout the United States, the younger members of the tribe began to express a pride in being "Indian" that they did not have before this time. This pride continued to grow among the young until enough of them convinced the tribal elders that it was time to come out of hiding and be counted among the "Indian" nations again. They were tired of reading that the tribe had been absorbed by other tribes such as their old enemy, the Tonica who called themselves the Tunica now. The elders finally agreed to move slowly and cautiously out of hiding and wanted to find their lost relatives from les Rapides, Second Village, and reunite the Nation once more under the newly chosen chief "John" Mayeux. It was under his slow and studied leadership that the tribe began its new Journey.

55

John Sitting Bear

When news surfaced that the AVOGEL were looking for their lost relatives, many people in Avoyelles Parish saw a chance to be classified as "Indian" to receive money and benefits from the U.S. Government. They even went so far as to falsify records to try and get their names on the AVOGEL rolls. Many succeeded at first; but, eventually were found out and forced to leave. There is still a movement by some people of Avoyelles Parish who do have "Indian" blood but who cannot prove it, and who belong to other tribes, are attempting to get their names on the AVOGEL rolls. Since the money and benefits did not come soon enough for these forgers and liars, they formed tribes of their own. The one thing that will prevent them from being recognized as AVOGEL by both the tribe and the Federal Government, is the fact that tribal affiliation is obtained from the mother and not the father. In other words, your mother's, mother's, mother, back to as long as records were kept or families known, had to be AVOGEL to belong to the AVOGEL

Tribe. The only other way was to be adopted into the Tribe and unless the mother was AVOGEL, the children would not inherit membership in the tribe. This has ALWAYS been the way of the AVOGEL.

In 1998, the AVOGEL tribe was incorporated and a great seal was developed to tell the story of the AVOGEL as a people. As of 29 July 2000, we applied to the Federal Government for formal Nation-to-Nation relationship between them and the AVOGEL Nation/ Tribe. We are still presently working on that process. Whether we succeed or not, makes no difference. We are the AVOGEL, we still exist as ourselves and have not been absorbed by any other "Indian" nations. We will continue to take care of our "People" (the AVOGEL) just as we have in the past. We do not NEED the United States Government to tell us who we are; we know who we are. We simply wish to establish a working relationship between our people and the people of the United States. In 2002, we were able to obtain land on which we have established our reservation. This land is located in Avoyelles Parish where our historic homeland existed. Here, we will stay, and hopefully grow in numbers honoring our ancestors and moving into the future with our heads high, and in dignity .

Our people have fought in American Wars for the security and peace for America because we are Americans too. We still defend this country, as in the old days, for it is still our country even though we are reduced to only a small reservation. We honor our veterans, living and dead, men and women! Our goal is to maintain who we were and who we are into the future.

Chasse generale du
Chovrcuil

Femme et Fille

Indian woman and daughter

John Sitting Bear

Naturels en Eté.

CHAPTER 3
The Customs and Laws

AVOGEL Tribal Law

No man owns the land. The land belongs to the Tribe, which keeps other Tribes off of it. A man uses only as much land as he tills, or occupies with his house or his field. When he ceases to occupy or till the land, it goes back to the Tribe, to be allotted to another Tribesman.

No man owns the wood of the forest; or the water of the rivers, or the soil of the earth. He did not make them, they are the harvest of the land that belongs to the whole People; and only so much of them are his as he can gather with his own hands and use in his own home.

The wild plants are under the same law, but a man may claim certain forage crops, such as wild rice, by establishing his owner mark around a reasonable area before it is ripe to cut. However, the Tribal Council shall be judge as to the reasonableness of his claim.

No man owns game or wild animals, for these are the produce of the land that belongs to the nation only so much of them is his as he can effectively and lawfully possess with his own hands. In some cases, he may hold the sole right to capture eagles or hawks within a certain area.

All men are free and equal, and have a right to pursue happiness in their own way so long as it does not interfere with the rights of others.

Every man must treat with respect, all such things as are sacred to other people, whether he understands them or not.

Every person who is sick, or helpless, due to old age, or infirm, has a right to the protection and support of the Tribe, because in the days of their strength, they also contributed to the common wealth. This protection is also extended to those who are a special gift from the Creator, those who have diminished mental abilities.

No one is to say anything that is not true. Once a person's word has been given; it cannot be taken back. Words must be carefully considered before being spoken so as not to be guilty of stating a falsehood. It is for this reason that people are encouraged to speak only when they have something important to say that they know or believe to be truthful.

Laws are decided upon by tradition. Punishment for breach of any law is meted out by the Chief with the advice of the Tribal

Council. In all cases, public opinion is the most important thing in deciding on the punishment. In some cases, payment for damages is imposed; or in rare cases, physical punishment; in extreme cases, death or banishment.

Upon rising in the morning, each person is to thank the Creator for another day. Each person is to live each day as if it is the last, for it may turn out that way.

Each person or the head of a family or clan will thank the Creator for each meal by casting a morsel of meat into the fire and say, "Creator, partake with us."

Be careful to those who are in your power. It is the part of a coward to torture a prisoner or ill-treat those that are helpless before you, excluding prisoners of war .It is the part of the Chief to take care of the weak, the sick, the old, and the helpless.

Show respect to all; but grovel to none.

It is more honorable to give than to receive. Those who have, must always share with those who need. The greatness of a person is measured by how much he gives away and not how much he has. Service to the People is the highest honor a person may attain.

Do not speak of the dead except to recall their good deeds.

When you arrive at a strange camp or village, first pay your respects to the Chief before you call on your friends or family of a lesser rank. It may be that the Chief does not wish you to be received at all.

When you leave a camp, clean up all you rubbish, burn or bury it. Do not go around polluting the land or destroying its beauty .

Always give a word or sign of salute when meeting or passing a friend, or even a stranger, if in a lonely place.

John Sitting Bear

A man is bound by his promise with a bond that cannot be broken except by permission of the other party .

Always give your guest the place of honor in the lodge, at the feast, and serve him in reasonable ways. Never sit while your guest stands.

Protect your guest as one of the family; feed his horse, and beat your dogs if they harm his dog.

Do not trouble your guest with many questions about himself; he will tell you what he wishes you to know when he is ready.

In another man's lodge, follow his customs, not your own.

Never worry your host with your troubles unless he specifically asks you to tell him what bothers you.

Give your host a gift when he receives you.

Say, "thank you" for every gift, however small.

Compliment your host, even if you must strain the facts to do so. Never come between anyone and the fire.

Never walk between persons talking. Never interrupt persons talking! Never force your conversation on anyone.

Let silence be your motto until duty bids you speak. Speak softly.

Do not touch live coals with a steel knife or any sharp steel. Do not break a marrow bone in the lodge; it is unlucky .

Celibacy is discouraged. When a man weds, he moves into his wife's lodge and takes care of her parents and becomes a son to them.

Children inherit from their mother and not their father. A child inherits his mother's clan, and people. He/she honors his/her father's people.

John Sitting Bear

Once chosen as a chief; that person is always a chief unto death. If another leader of the people strongly disagrees with the Chief, he/she and his/her followers may leave and form their own tribal group. They are then on their own and are no longer a part of the nation but are now a different nation/people.

Children should not be beaten or struck as a means of discipling. They are to be taught by example of the elders. A child may be restrained if he/she attempts to do something that will permanently, harm him/her or the People. No one, not even a child, may ever be permitted to harm the People. The well being of the People is more important than the well being of a single individual.

False accusation of another person is a lie and is the most grievous wrong since it ultimately endangers the People. Punishment for such as act usually ends in banishment; for that person can never be trusted again.

Only the Chief with the advice of the Tribal Council and Elders may allow someone who has been banished to return to the People.

Persons who wish to marry , must marry outside of their respective clans so that children will be healthy and strong. Marriages outside of the Tribe are also encouraged to foster healthy children and friendly ties to other Tribes.

When war is declared, each male member must decide if he will fight or not. If it is his decision not to fight, he must be prepared to stay behind and protect the women and children from enemies while the other warriors are gone to battle.

It is the women's council that decides if a war is to be fought and it is the men's council that plans on how to fight the war. This is done this way since it is the women who will have to see to the care of the children and the continuation of the Tribe if the husband is killed in battle.

John Sitting Bear

When visiting an unknown tribe or a tribe known not to be friendly to the People, a tribal emissary will carry a white feather on a staff which indicates that the person is coming in a good way with friendly intentions. This person is allowed to enter the village unharmed and appear before the Chief.

Government Organization

The government of the Tribe begins with the People. The People select a Tribal Council to advise the Chief. The Tribal Council is formed with the Elders of the Tribe, in whom the People have confidence as being wise. The Chief makes all final decisions on matters affecting the Tribe.

When a person is accused of wrong doing, the Chief acts as Judge and the Tribal Council acts as jury .The Chief has the final decision as to punishment of the person, if the person is found "guilty" by the Tribal Council. Punishment is determined by traditional law. Any decision of the Tribal Council may be appealed to the Chief who has the final say in what is to be done. Only the Chief can over-rule the Tribal Council. The Tribal Council elects the Chief when there is a vacancy. The Tribal Council selects candidates for War Chief, Peace Chief, Leader of the Dog Soldiers, Buzzard Men, and Shirt Wearers. The Tribal

Council recommends approval or disapproval of warrior societies, and establishment of Clans. Clans are composed of persons who are closely related.

The women of the Tribe form a women's council which decides if the Tribe is to go to war or not. If the tribe is attacked without warning or if enemies are spied approaching, it is the duty of all of the People to fight and protect the People. Even women can be warriors, although this is not normally done since women give life. They are allowed to do whatever is necessary to protect themselves, the children, and any others of the people who are in danger of being killed.

Burial Customs

When a person dies, the family turns the body over to the Buzzard Men to prepare the body for the burial ceremony. The Buzzard Men cut bits of hair from the body and nails, and place these with items used by the deceased (such as a medicine pouch), in a bag that a selected member of the family will take care of during the year of mourning. This bag is believed to possess the soul of the deceased.

The body is washed and wrapped in animal skin or cloth and brought to the burial grounds. At the burial grounds, the body is placed on a scaffold about six feet off the ground. Personal possessions are also placed with the individual. These are items that it is believed the dead will need in the after life. The body and scaffold is blessed with smoke, and around the scaffold is built a six foot high palisade wall with an opening to the South, where the soul goes after death.

John Sitting Bear

During the year following the death, the soul bearer, cares for the bag and places it on a tripod in a place of honor in the house. It is brought to Tribal gatherings and celebrations too. At the end of the year, the bag is placed on the scaffold and the scaffold is burned; thereby releasing the soul and the family says its good-byes. The ashes and any bones that are left are gathered and buried in a mound that has been set aside to receive the remains.

This was the way our People were buried in the old days. Today, since most of the People are of the Catholic Church, we have traditional church services; but, we still bless the body with smoke and a relative or the Chief offers a pipe at the exposition of the body and at the gravesite. This is our way today.

Marriage Customs

When a young man wanted to marry a young woman, he would give presents to the girl's parents and ask their permission to marry their daughter. If the gifts were accepted by the parents, then the young man had permission to ask the young girl to marry him. If she refused, the gifts were kept by the parents, and the young man had to look elsewhere. If they young woman accepted the proposal of marriage, then plans for the wedding were made. The woman would begin building a house for herself and her new husband near her parents' house. Other women relatives would help her build the house. She would make her wedding dress, and a pair of moccasins for her husband. On the wedding day, the two were brought together with the whole village as witnesses. The young man and his family would have gone hunting and would have prepared a feast for the village celebration

79

after the ceremony. The ceremony was usually officiated by the Chief who would speak of the duties that a husband had toward his wife and what duties a wife had toward her husband. After the two exchanged gifts that they had made for the other, and expressed their desire to be husband and wife, the wife would introduce her new husband to the People and the husband would then introduce his new wife to the People. With this completed, the dancing and feasting would begin and continue until dusk, at which time the young married couple was excused to begin their honeymoon.

If for some reason, after they had been married, the couple found that they were not happy with their choice, they were allowed to separate without recrimination from anyone. The wife owned all that the couple had accumulated and she would give her ex- husband whatever she felt he should keep. If they had children, the children would stay with the mother and the father would continue to see to their needs and help raise the children. Both were allowed to remarry if they found someone else.

Although a man could have more than one wife, it was very rare that this occurred. However, a man could have only as many wives as he could take care of properly. Fidelity to one's spouse was very important. The punishment for taking another's spouse was banishment. The children, if any, were then raised by the Tribe.

Making of Relatives

There were rare times when a person was adopted as one of the People. This was done, usually, because the individual had done something that was extraordinarily beneficial to the Tribe. This of course had to be done with the approval of all of the People.

In the making of relatives, a gift of corn was brought by the person being adopted and a special ceremony was conducted by the holy man of the Tribe, after which a great feast was enjoyed by all.

Groups of people and even another Tribe could be adopted also to foster close ties between these people and our People. Once the ceremony was over, these People were considered as blood relatives and were given all the benefits and rights of any member of the Tribe.

CHAPTER 4
Stories That Teach

Indigenous People have many stories to tell. Most of them are animal stories similar to those of Rabelais of France and Aesop of Greece. These stories were not only entertaining; but also taught a lesson, usually intended for young people. At the end of the day, people used to like to gather around the fire and tell these stories. Although some stories are usually identified with a certain Tribe, no one can say for sure where these stories originated. There was no copyright for story telling. Listed below are some stories that were told around AVOGEL campfires. There

John Sitting Bear

were many, many more; but these will serve as an example of the kind of stories that were told.

How Skunk Got His Stripe

In the time of long ago, in the time of the Grandfather's Grandfathers, before man was made, there were only animals and they could talk. One of these animals was Skunk (Koni -in the Trade Language). Koni was the most beautiful animal in the forest and he was all white with a fluffy , beautiful tail. Unfortunately Koni knew that he was beautiful and made fun of all of the other animals. Koni had no friends because of his attitude at being the most beautiful. He used to go around telling others, "You are not as beautiful as I. You are ugly. You're lucky I stay around you. I'm glad I'm not ugly like you." Because of all of this bragging, Koni was lonely and friendless; but he could not bring himself to stop his bragging.

One day he was walking down a road with a tall, old tree and a nest at the top of the tree. He heard some noise coming from the nest and decided to investigate since he had nothing better

85

to do. When he got to the top, he saw baby owls (Ofunlo -in the Trade Language) in the nest. Well, I don't know about you, but, baby Ofunlo are not exactly the cutest babies in the wild. Well, Koni could not help himself and started picking on the babies. He said, "My gracious, you are so ugly! I cannot believe how ugly you look. You 're so ugly, I couldn't even think of eating you for a snack; you turn my stomach!" The babies were very hurt by Koni ' s words and began to cry and cry very loud.

Off in the distance, Koni saw mother Ofunlo coming toward the nest. She had heard her babies crying and was coming to see what was wrong. Koni decided to leave immediately and down he went and away down the road he ran! When mother Ofunlo got to the nest, she asked her babies what was wrong and they told her how Koni had been mean to them. This made mother very angry with Koni. She decided to find him and punish him for what he had done.

She flew off into the distance and followed the road until she say Koni and then swooped down and caught him in her talons. Now she was trying to decide how best to punish him for his mischief. Off to the West she saw a great forest fire, blazing hot. She decided to drop Knoi in the fire and teach him a lesson. So, off she flew and dropped Koni right in the middle of the hottest part of the fire.

It was not long until she heard Koni crying for help, "Help me, help me, I'm burning up and I'm afraid to die!" Well, mother Ofunlo did not want to kill Koni, she only wanted to teach him a lesson. So, she swooped down and grabbed him in her talons again and flew out of the fire towards a lake she knew. All she could see of Koni was a black cloud of smoke and he was coughing badly. When she got over the lake, she dropped him in and flew away. Finally, Koni swam to the edge of the lake and crawled out onto the bank, choking and sputtering. Mother Ofunlo was satisfied that she had taught Koni a lesson and that he would not bother her little ones again.

As Koni got up, he noticed that he was no longer white, but black, where his fur had gotten burned, except for a white stripe up the middle of his back which had not been burned by the fire. In fact, since then, it is said that if you get close enough to Koni, you can still smell that burnt fur smell from when he was burned in the fire.

How Possum Got His Grin

There came a time of great drought in the land and all the animals were getting thin and were very hungry .One day deer (Issi -in the Trade Language) saw opossum (SHUKAnTA -in the Trade Language). SHUKAnTA was big and fat unlike all the other animals and Issi was wondering how he was so well fed.

Issi decided to confront SHUKAnTA and find out where he was getting his food to be so fat. He asked him and SHUKAnTA said, "I eat persimmons like the ones in that tree over there. I tell you what. Go up to that small rise and come running down as fast as you can and butt the tree and then you'll be able to eat all the persimmons you want." Well, Issi thought it over for a minute and being hungry like he was, decided to try it out. He went up the rise and then started running toward the tree as fast as he could and butted his head against the trunk of the tree. He hit it so hard that he knocked himself out cold; but did succeed in shaking the tree so hard that all the persimmons fell to the ground. SHUKAnTA was laughing so hard when he saw what happened that his mouth split form ear to ear and that is why today you can see the big grin on the face of SHUKAnTA. When he finally stopped laughing, he gobbled up all the persimmons that were on the ground. Issi had been fooled and awoke still hungry, and feeling very foolish.

John Sitting Bear

BIBLIOGRAPHY

1. The History of Louisiana , M. LePage DuPratz, Claitor's Publishing Division" 3165 S. Acadian at 1-10, P.O. Box 239, Baton Rouge, La. 70821, Reprinted 1972, Limited Edition of 500 copies.

2. The Historic Indian Tribes of Louisiana From 154f to the Present. Fred B. Kniffen, Hiram F. Gregory , & George A. Stokes, Louisiana State University Press, Baton Rouge, La. and London, England, 1994.

3. Rencontres sur le Mississippi 1682- 1763, Gail Alexander Buzhardt and Margaret Hawthorne, Published for the Mississippi Dept. of Archives and

History, University Press of Mississippi, Jackson, Mississippi, 1993.

4. On The Tunica Trail, Third Ed., Jeffrey P. Brain (Peabody and Essex Museum), and Bill Day (Director, Tunica-Bi10xi Cultural and Historic Preservation), Dept. of Culture, Recreation, and Tourism, Louisiana Archaeological Survey and Antiquities Division, U.S. Dept. of the Interior, Washington, D.C. 20241, 1994.

5. Indian Tribes of the Lower Mississippi Valley and Adjacent Coast of the Gulf of Mexico, John R. Swanton, Dover Publications, Inc. Mineola, New York, 1998.

6. Atlas of the North American Indian, Carl Waldman, Maps and Illustrations by Molly Braun, Facts on File, Inc., New York, V 01.1, 1947.

7. The Gospel of the Redman, Ernest Thompson Seton and Julia M. Seton, Seton Village, Santa Fe, New Mexico, 1966.

8. The Five Civilized Tribes, Grant_Foreman, University of Oklahoma Press, Norman, Publishing Division of the University, 1934.

9. The Indian Tribes of North America., John R. Swanton, Smithsonian Institution Press, Washington and London, 1969.

10. North American Indians, A Comprehensive Account. Second Ed. , Alice B. Kehoe, Prentice Hall, Englewood Cliffs, New Jersey, 1992.

11. Crazy Horse, The Strange Man of the Oglalas, Mari Sandoz, University of Nebraska Press, Lincoln and London, 1942.

12. The Genealogy Forum: Native American Resource Center: Southeastern U.S., http:// genealogyforum.corn/gfaol/resource/ NA!gfna0002.htrn, p.5, 2002.

13. Interview: Bertaha Jones Bonton (112 years old) and Lelia Bonton James (77 years old), 11.16 A.M., CT, 360 Overton St., Marksville, La.

About the Author

He has been Chief of the Avogel since the death of his mother in 1975. As a child he was taught the ways of his ancestors, primarily by his mother and the tribal story teller. His father taught him how to hunt and fish like the tribe did in the "Old Days"! His grandmother "Alice" showed him the healing herbs and how to use them. It was his Aunt "Nini" who instilled the pride of his heritage, but with a warning about mentioning it to outsiders. She reminded him of relatives who had been murdered for simply "Being" Avogel! His service in the U.S. Air Force brought him into contact with other indigenous people who had similar experiences and who convinced him that it was safer now to admit to being who he was. Yes, there still were risks, but they showed him how to fight back in today's world & society for the good of his people. It is time for the world to know that the Avogel still exist and have not been "Absorbed" or "Cease to Exist" as some claim!

www.ingramcontent.com/pod-product-compliance
Lightning Source LLC
Chambersburg PA
CBHW031630110626
46523CB00055B/333